MW01125089

YOUR COMPLETE SAGITTARIUS 2024 PERSONAL HOROSCOPE

Monthly Astrological Prediction Forecast Readings of
Every Zodiac Astrology Sun Star Signs- Love,
Romance, Money, Finances, Career, Health, Travel,
Spirituality.

Iris Quinn

Alpha Zuriel Publishing

Your Complete Sagittarius 2024 Personal Horoscope/ Iris Quinn. -- 1st ed.

"In the dance of the planets, we find the rhythms of life. Astrology reminds us that we are all connected to the greater universe, and our actions have ripple effects throughout the cosmos."

— IRIS QUINN

CONTENTS

CHAPTER ONE

SAGITTARIUS PROFILE

- Constellation: Sagittarius
- Zodiac symbol: Archer
- Date: November 22 - December 21
- Element: Fire
- Ruling Planet: Jupiter
- Career Planet: Mars
- Love Planet: Venus
- Money Planet: Jupiter
- Planet of Fun, Entertainment, Creativity, and Speculations: Sun
- Planet of Health and Work: Mercury
- Planet of Home and Family Life: Moon
- Planet of Spirituality: Neptune
- Planet of Travel, Education, Religion, and Philosophy: Jupiter

  Colors:
- Colors: Purple, Blue

- Colors that promote love, romance, and social harmony: Green, Turquoise
- Color that promotes earning power: Yellow

Gem: Turquoise
Metals: Tin
Scent: Lavender
Birthstone: Turquoise

Qualities:
• Quality: Mutable (represents adaptability)
• Quality most needed for balance: Discipline

Strongest Virtues:
• Adventurous nature
• Optimism
• Honesty
• Independence
• Enthusiasm

Deepest Need: Freedom

Characteristics to Avoid:
• Impulsiveness
• Restlessness
• Carelessness
• Insensitivity

Signs of Greatest Overall Compatibility:

- Aries
- Leo
- Libra
- Aquarius

Signs of Greatest Overall Incompatibility:

- Taurus
- Cancer
- Virgo
- Scorpio
- Capricorn
- Pisces

- Sign Most Supportive for Career Advancement: Aries
- Sign Most Supportive for Emotional Well-being: Leo
- Sign Most Supportive Financially: Capricorn
- Sign Best for Marriage and/or Partnerships: Gemini
- Sign Most Supportive for Creative Projects: Aquarius
- Best Sign to Have Fun With: Leo

Signs Most Supportive in Spiritual Matters:

- Aries

- Leo
- Scorpio
- Aquarius

Best Day of the Week: Thursday

SAGITTARIUS TRAITS

- Adventurous and free-spirited nature
- Optimistic and positive outlook on life
- Honest and straightforward in communication
- Independent and self-reliant
- Enthusiastic and energetic in pursuing goals
- Open-minded and willing to explore new ideas.
- Restless and prone to impulsiveness at times

PERSONALITY OF SAGITTARIUS

Sagittarius individuals are characterized by their vibrant and expansive personality. They possess a strong sense of adventure and an insatiable curiosity that drives them to explore the world around them. They have an optimistic outlook on life and a natural enthusiasm that is infectious to those around them. Sagittarians are known for their honesty and straightforwardness, often speaking their minds with no filter. They value their freedom and independence and are not afraid to go against the grain to pursue their own truth.

With their abundant physical energy, Sagittarians are always on the move, seeking new experiences and embracing challenges. They have a natural zest for life and a genuine love for exploration and discovery. Their adventurous spirit and open-mindedness make them great travel companions and lifelong learners. They have a deep-seated need for personal growth and are constantly seeking to expand their horizons through education, travel, and spiritual pursuits.

Sagittarius individuals have a natural charisma and charm that draws people to them. They are known for their sense of humor and infectious laughter, making them the life of the party. They have a genuine interest in others and are skilled at engaging in meaningful conversations. However, their love for freedom and independence can sometimes make them appear commitment-phobic or restless in relationships. They crave intellectual stimulation and need a partner who can keep up with their adventurous spirit.

While their optimism and enthusiasm are admirable traits, Sagittarians can sometimes be overly idealistic and prone to making impulsive decisions. They may struggle with commitment and maintaining focus on long-term goals. It is important for them to balance their desire for freedom with a sense of responsibility and commitment to avoid spreading themselves too thin.

Overall, Sagittarius individuals bring a sense of adventure, enthusiasm, and open-mindedness to any relationship or situation. Their vibrant personality and love for exploration make them natural explorers and seekers of truth.

WEAKNESSES OF SAGITTARIUS

Sagittarius individuals, with their adventurous and enthusiastic nature, bring a vibrant energy to any situation. They have a zest for life that is contagious and a genuine desire to explore the world around them. However, like all zodiac signs, Sagittarius has their share of weaknesses that can arise in certain circumstances.

One of the weaknesses of Sagittarius is their restlessness. They possess a strong need for freedom and independence, always seeking new experiences and adventures. This restlessness can sometimes lead to impulsive decision-making, as they chase after the next exciting opportunity without fully considering the consequences. While their spontaneous nature can be thrilling, it can also result in hasty choices that they may later regret.

Another aspect of Sagittarius' personality that can be challenging is their bluntness. They are known for their honesty and straightforwardness, often speaking their mind without filter. While this quality can be refreshing and genuine, it can also come across as tactless and hurtful to those who are more sensitive.

Sagittarians may need to exercise more diplomacy and consider the impact of their words on others.

Patience is not always a strong suit for Sagittarius. Their natural sense of urgency and desire for instant gratification can make them easily frustrated when things don't progress as quickly as they would like. This impatience can sometimes hinder their ability to persevere through challenges or stick with long-term projects.

When it comes to commitment, Sagittarius individuals value their personal freedom and independence. This can make them hesitant to fully commit in relationships or feel trapped in long-term commitments. They may need space and flexibility to explore their individual interests, which can sometimes create challenges in finding a balance between personal freedom and partnership.

Lastly, Sagittarius individuals can be overly optimistic at times, overlooking potential risks or challenges. Their natural optimism can be inspiring, but it can also lead to unrealistic expectations and disappointment when reality doesn't align with their grand visions.

It's important to remember that these weaknesses are not inherent flaws, but rather aspects of Sagittarius' personality that may require awareness and growth. By understanding their tendencies and working on self-improvement, Sagittarius individuals can harness their strengths and navigate their weaknesses to lead fulfilling lives.

RELATIONSHIP COMPATIBILITY WITH SAGITTARIUS

Based only on their Sun signs, this is how Sagittarius interacts with others. These are the compatibility interpretations for all 12 potential Sagittarius combinations. This is a limited and insufficient method of determining compatibility.

However, Sun-sign compatibility remains the foundation for overall harmony in a relationship.

The general rule is that yin and yang do not get along. Yin complements yin, and yang complements yang. While yin and yang partnerships can be successful, they require more effort. Earth and water zodiac signs are both Yin. Yang is represented by the fire and air zodiac signs.

Sagittarius (Yang) and Aries (Yang):

When Sagittarius and Aries come together, their fiery personalities create a passionate and dynamic relationship. Both signs are adventurous, independent, and enthusiastic, which fuels their shared sense of

10

exploration and excitement. They thrive on taking risks and embarking on new adventures together, constantly pushing each other out of their comfort zones. Their connection is built on a strong foundation of mutual respect and admiration for each other's individuality.

Sagittarius (Yang) and Taurus (Yin):

Sagittarius and Taurus have contrasting energies, with Sagittarius being spontaneous and adventurous, while Taurus is more grounded and focused on stability. Their relationship can be a balancing act between Sagittarius' need for freedom and Taurus' desire for security. However, if they can find common ground and appreciate each other's strengths, they can create a relationship that combines adventure and stability. Taurus can provide grounding and support for Sagittarius, while Sagittarius can inspire Taurus to embrace new experiences and broaden their horizons.

Sagittarius (Yang) and Gemini (Yang)

When Sagittarius and Gemini come together, their intellectual connection is strong and stimulating. Both signs are curious, open-minded, and love to engage in deep conversations. They thrive on mental stimulation and can spend hours exploring various topics and ideas together. Their relationship is filled with wit, humor, and a constant exchange of ideas. However, they may need to be mindful of maintaining a balance between intellectual connection and emotional intimacy.

Sagittarius (Yang) and Cancer (Yin):

Sagittarius and Cancer have different approaches to life and relationships. Sagittarius is outgoing and adventurous, while Cancer is nurturing and focused on emotional security. Their compatibility may require understanding and compromise to bridge these differences. Cancer can teach Sagittarius the value of emotional depth and stability, while Sagittarius can inspire Cancer to embrace new experiences and expand their horizons.

Sagittarius (Yang) and Leo (Yang):

When Sagittarius and Leo come together, their energy is fiery and dynamic. Both signs are enthusiastic, optimistic, and love to be the center of attention. They enjoy each other's company and can create a vibrant and exciting relationship. Their shared passion for life and adventure can lead to a fulfilling partnership filled with mutual support and encouragement. However, they may need to be mindful of their egos and avoid power struggles, as both signs have strong personalities.

Sagittarius (Yang) and Virgo (Yin):

Sagittarius and Virgo have contrasting energies, with Sagittarius being spontaneous and Virgo being practical and analytical. Their compatibility lies in their ability to appreciate and learn from each other's strengths. Sagittarius can inspire Virgo to embrace spontaneity and take risks, while Virgo can provide stability and practicality to Sagittarius' adventurous nature. They may need to find a balance between Sagittarius' need for freedom and Virgo's desire for routine and order.

Sagittarius (Yang) and Libra (Yang):

Sagittarius and Libra share a love for adventure, intellectual pursuits, and social connections. They both enjoy exploring new places, meeting new people, and engaging in meaningful conversations. Their relationship is characterized by harmony, mutual understanding, and a deep sense of friendship. They can support and encourage each other's personal growth and share a strong bond based on shared values and intellectual connection.

Sagittarius (Yang) and Scorpio (Yin):

Sagittarius and Scorpio have contrasting energies, with Sagittarius being outgoing and Scorpio being introspective and intense. Their compatibility lies in their ability to complement each other's strengths. Sagittarius can bring lightness and optimism to Scorpio's intense nature, while Scorpio can provide depth and emotional intimacy to Sagittarius' adventurous spirit. They may need to navigate their differences and communicate openly to find a balance between freedom and emotional connection.

Sagittarius (Yang) and Sagittarius (Yang):

When two Sagittarius individuals come together, their shared energy creates a relationship filled with enthusiasm, adventure, and a love for life. They understand and appreciate each other's need for freedom and exploration. Their connection is built on mutual respect and a shared zest for discovering new experiences. However, they may need to be mindful of maintaining a sense of stability and commitment within their relationship, as their desire for independence can sometimes overshadow the need for emotional connection.

Sagittarius (Yang) and Capricorn (Yin):

Sagittarius and Capricorn have contrasting energies, with Sagittarius being spontaneous and Capricorn being disciplined and focused on long-term goals. Their compatibility lies in their ability to learn from each other and find a balance between adventure and stability. Capricorn can provide grounding and practicality to Sagittarius' adventurous nature, while Sagittarius can inspire Capricorn to embrace new experiences and find joy in the present moment.

Sagittarius (Yang) and Aquarius (Yang):

Sagittarius and Aquarius share a love for intellectual pursuits, freedom, and social connections. They both value independence and have a strong desire to make a positive impact on the world. Their relationship is characterized by intellectual stimulation, shared ideals, and a deep sense of friendship. They can support each other's personal growth and engage in meaningful conversations. However, they may need to be mindful of maintaining emotional intimacy and addressing any tendency to prioritize individual freedom over the needs of the relationship.

Sagittarius (Yang) and Pisces (Yin):

Sagittarius and Pisces have different approaches to life and relationships. Sagittarius is adventurous and optimistic, while Pisces is intuitive and sensitive. Their compatibility lies in their ability to appreciate and learn from each other's strengths. Sagittarius can bring excitement and optimism to Pisces' emotional depth, while Pisces can provide empathy and spiritual connection to Sagittarius' quest for knowledge and experience. They may need to find a balance between adventure and emotional intimacy in their relationship.

LOVE AND PASSION

Love and passion are intrinsic to the Sagittarius personality. Sagittarius individuals approach love with a sense of adventure, enthusiasm, and an open heart. They are passionate and romantic, seeking experiences that ignite their spirit and expand their horizons.

In relationships, Sagittarius seeks a partner who can keep up with their energetic and adventurous nature. They are drawn to those who share their love for exploration, intellectual stimulation, and freedom. Sagittarius values their independence and needs a partner who understands and respects their need for personal space and individual growth.

When Sagittarius falls in love, they do so wholeheartedly. They are generous, expressive, and passionate lovers who enjoy showering their partner with affection and excitement. Their love is like a blazing fire, burning with intensity and desire.

Sagittarius individuals are not afraid to take risks in love. They are willing to embark on new experiences, whether it be traveling to exotic destinations, trying new activities, or engaging in deep philosophical conversations. They thrive on the thrill of the unknown and are always seeking to expand their understanding of love and relationships.

However, Sagittarius can sometimes struggle with commitment. Their love for freedom and exploration may make them hesitant to settle down or feel tied down in a traditional relationship. They value their independence and may need a partner who can provide them with the space they need while still nurturing a deep emotional connection.

In the realm of passion, Sagittarius is known for their fiery and adventurous nature. They approach intimacy with enthusiasm, spontaneity, and a sense of playfulness. They enjoy exploring different facets of their sexuality and are open to trying new things to keep the passion alive.

Sagittarius individuals value honesty and transparency in their relationships. They appreciate a partner who can match their intellectual curiosity, engage in stimulating conversations, and provide them with emotional support. Mutual respect and trust are crucial for Sagittarius to feel secure and deeply connected in a romantic relationship.

Overall, love and passion are integral parts of the Sagittarius experience. They bring a sense of adventure, enthusiasm, and a willingness to explore the depths of love and intimacy. With the right partner who understands and embraces their free-spirited nature, Sagittarius can create a love story that is filled with excitement, growth, and a shared journey of discovery.

MARRIAGE

Sagittarius individuals are generally supportive of marriage, but they prioritize ensuring their financial stability before making a commitment. They understand the importance of a solid foundation and want to be able to provide for their partner and future family.

However, Sagittarius individuals should be mindful of their tendency to engage in disputes and criticize their partner. They need to temper these tendencies to avoid weakening their partner's morale and jeopardizing the relationship. Open and respectful communication is essential for them to maintain a harmonious and thriving marriage.

In general, Sagittarius individuals strive to keep their marriage alive and flourishing. They bring their adventurous spirit and optimism into the relationship, infusing it with excitement and a constant desire for growth and exploration. They see marriage as an opportunity for personal and mutual development.

Sagittarius women are extremely adaptable and understand the importance of balancing work and family duties. They are organized and efficient, bringing a sense of order and effectiveness to their marriage. They approach their marital tasks with the best possible attitude, seeking to create a harmonious and supportive home environment.

Sagittarius men are dedicated workers who value their roles as husbands and fathers. They take pride in their responsibilities and are committed to creating a loving and nurturing family environment. They reject sexism and believe in equal partnership, ensuring that their spouse never performs more than their fair share.

If Sagittarius individuals find that disagreements in their marriage are insurmountable, they will not hesitate to consider ending the relationship. They value their freedom and personal growth, and they believe that it is essential to be in a marriage where both partners can thrive and be true to themselves.

Overall, a Sagittarius marriage is characterized by adventure, growth, and a shared commitment to personal development. With their positive outlook on life, Sagittarius individuals create a marriage filled with optimism, enthusiasm, and a constant pursuit of new experiences.

CHAPTER TWO

SAGITTARIUS 2024 HOROSCOPE

Overview Sagittarius 2024

Sagittarius, the year 2024 will be a year of exploration, growth, and self-discovery for you. The planetary movements throughout the year indicate a time of opportunities and challenges that will shape your life in profound ways. The alignment of the Sun, Mercury, Venus, Mars, and Jupiter will play a crucial role in various aspects of your life, including your career, relationships, health, and personal development. Let's delve deeper into what the year has in store for you.

The year kicks off with a burst of energy in your career sector. The conjunction between Mercury and Uranus in Taurus in May is a cosmic signal for innovation. This is the time to think outside the box. Your creativity will be your currency, so invest it wisely. New ideas will flow, and you may find yourself in the midst of groundbreaking projects. However, with great power comes great responsibility. The square between Mars and Pluto in June is a reminder to tread carefully. Workplace conflicts and power struggles may arise. It is essential to maintain your integrity and stay true to your values.

As you move into the second half of the year, the financial aspect takes center stage. The sextile between Venus and Chiron in June is a healing balm to any financial wounds you may have. This is a period of financial recuperation. Reassess your financial goals, and don't be afraid to make necessary adjustments. Networking is key during this period. The quintile between Venus and the True Node in June suggests that making the right connections can open doors to financial opportunities.

In the realm of relationships and social life, the square between Venus and Neptune in June indicates a period of confusion or misunderstanding. You may find yourself questioning your relationships or feeling unsure about your feelings. It's important to communicate clearly and honestly during this time and to seek clarity when needed. Remember, every relationship has its ups and downs. It's how you navigate these challenges that truly matters.

The sextile between Mercury and the True Node in June suggests that communication will be key during this time. Whether it's a romantic relationship, a friendship, or a professional connection, make sure to express your thoughts and feelings clearly. This is also a great time to expand your social circle and meet new people.

In terms of health and wellness, the sesquiquadrate between the Sun and Chiron in June suggests a time of healing and recovery. This is a good time to focus on self-care and wellness practices. Whether it's starting a new fitness regimen, adopting a healthier diet, or seeking therapy, take steps to improve your health and well-being.

The latter part of the year brings vitality. The sextile between the Sun and Chiron in June also indicates a period of high energy and vitality. Use this energy to pursue activities that you enjoy and that contribute to your health. This could be anything from hiking in nature to taking up a new sport.

The year 2024 will be a significant year for your spiritual growth and personal development. The quintile between Jupiter and Saturn in May suggests a time of spiritual learning and growth. You may find yourself drawn to philosophical or spiritual studies that can help you understand the world in a deeper way.

The conjunction between Venus and Pluto in July suggests a time of deep transformation and personal growth. This is a time to embrace change and to allow yourself to grow and evolve. Whether it's changing old habits, adopting new perspectives, or embarking on a new journey, embrace the transformations that come your way.

The quintile between Jupiter and the True Node in December indicates a period of spiritual alignment and purpose. You may find a greater sense of purpose and direction in your life, and your actions may be guided by a higher calling. This is a time to align your actions with your spiritual beliefs and values.

The semi-square between Mercury and Neptune in May, and the square between Sun and Neptune in December, suggest periods of confusion and uncertainty. These times may challenge your beliefs and force you to question your assumptions. However, these periods of uncertainty can also lead to greater clarity and understanding. Use these times to reflect on your beliefs and to seek deeper truths.

Sagittarius, 2024 is a mosaic of experiences. With its ups and downs, it promises to be a year that will leave an indelible mark on your soul. Your career will see waves of creativity, but it's essential to navigate them with wisdom. Financially, the year holds promise, but it requires shrewd management and making connections that align with your goals.

In relationships, communication will be your anchor. It's a year to forge bonds that resonate with your inner being. Your health and wellness need attention, and integrating practices that nourish your soul will be beneficial.

Spiritually, this year is a journey within. It's a quest for higher wisdom and embracing the metamorphosis that is bound to come.

As you traverse through the days and months of 2024, remember that the stars are your allies. Listen to their whispers, dance to their rhythm but never lose sight of the inner flame that guides you.

May 2024 be a year where you soar to new heights, dive into new depths, and embrace the boundless possibilities that await.

January 2024

Horoscope

In January 2024, Sagittarius individuals will experience a dynamic and transformative period. The planetary aspects indicate a mix of challenges and opportunities, urging Sagittarians to embrace change and personal growth. The month begins with a square aspect between Venus in Sagittarius and Saturn in Pisces, highlighting potential conflicts between personal desires and responsibilities. This can lead to a sense of frustration and limitations. However, it also presents an opportunity for Sagittarians to find a balance between their aspirations and practical obligations.

On January 3rd, Venus forms a quincunx aspect with Jupiter, emphasizing the need for Sagittarians to make adjustments in their relationships and financial matters. Communication is crucial during this time, as Mercury quintiles Saturn, encouraging thoughtful and structured discussions. Additionally, Venus forms a sesquiquadrate aspect with the True Node, suggesting that Sagittarians may need to reevaluate their social connections and align themselves with individuals who share their long-term goals.

Mars, the planet of action and energy, semi-sextiles Pluto on January 3rd, stimulating a strong drive for personal transformation. This aspect empowers Sagittarians to release old patterns and embrace a more empowered and authentic version of themselves. The Sun quintiles Neptune on the same day, enhancing their intuition and creative expression.

Love

For Sagittarius, January 2024 presents an exciting time for love and relationships. Venus, the planet of love, influences your sign, bringing a sense of passion and desire. However, the square aspect between Venus in Sagittarius and Saturn in Pisces on January 1st may introduce some tension and challenges in your relationships. It is crucial to communicate openly and honestly with your partner during this period to resolve any conflicts that may arise.

As the month progresses, the quincunx aspect between Venus in Sagittarius and Jupiter in Taurus on January 3rd could create a sense of imbalance and adjustment in your romantic life. This alignment may require you to reassess your priorities and find a harmonious balance between your personal desires and the needs of your partner.

Overall, the month holds potential for growth and deepening connections. The trine between Venus in Sagittarius and Chiron in Aries on January 11th brings emotional healing and the opportunity to strengthen the bonds with your loved ones. By focusing on open communication, trust, and understanding, Sagittarius can navigate the challenges and experience a fulfilling and passionate month in love.

Career

In terms of career, January 2024 brings promising opportunities for Sagittarius. The alignment between Mercury and Saturn on January 3rd indicates a period of mental focus and discipline. This aspect enables Sagittarius to approach their work with clarity and precision, allowing for effective decision-making and problem-solving.

The trine between Mars in Sagittarius and Jupiter in Taurus on January 12th amplifies your ambition and drive, providing favorable circumstances for career advancement. This alignment encourages Sagittarius to take calculated risks and pursue their goals with determination.

However, the square aspect between Venus in Sagittarius and Neptune in Pisces on January 19th may introduce some confusion and unrealistic expectations in the workplace. It is essential for Sagittarius to remain grounded and practical during this time, avoiding impulsive decisions or getting carried away by grandiose ideas.

Overall, January presents a month of progress and growth in your career. By utilizing your natural optimism, adaptability, and willingness to take on new challenges, Sagittarius can make significant strides and achieve professional success.

Finance

Financially, January 2024 offers both opportunities and challenges for Sagittarius. The semi-sextile aspect between Mars in Sagittarius and Pluto in Capricorn on January 3rd suggests the need for careful financial planning and resource management. It is crucial for Sagittarius to avoid impulsive spending and focus on long-term financial stability.

The biquintile aspect between Venus in Sagittarius and Jupiter in Taurus on January 8th brings positive energy and potential financial gains. This alignment favors investment opportunities and financial ventures. However, it is important to approach these opportunities with caution and thorough research to avoid unnecessary risks.

The semi-square aspect between Venus in Sagittarius and Pluto in Capricorn on January 10th may create some financial tension and power struggles. It is advisable for Sagittarius to practice financial prudence and avoid engaging in financial disputes during this period.

By maintaining a balanced approach to finances and exercising self-discipline, Sagittarius can navigate the challenges and make significant progress in their financial endeavors.

Health

January 2024 highlights the importance of self-care and overall well-being for Sagittarius. The square aspect between the Sun in Capricorn and Chiron in Aries on January 6th may bring up some emotional wounds and vulnerabilities. It is essential for Sagittarius to prioritize their mental and emotional health during this period and seek support from loved ones or professionals if needed.

The trine between Mars in Sagittarius and Jupiter in Taurus on January 12th enhances your physical vitality and energy levels. This alignment provides an excellent opportunity for Sagittarius to engage in physical activities, exercise routines, and adopt a healthier lifestyle overall.

However, the square aspect between the Sun in Aquarius and Jupiter in Taurus on January 27th may lead to some overindulgence or a lack of discipline in terms of health and well-being. It is crucial for Sagittarius to maintain a balanced approach and avoid excessive behaviors during this time.

By prioritizing self-care, maintaining a balanced lifestyle, and seeking emotional support when needed, Sagittarius can enjoy good health and vitality throughout January.

Travel

January 2024 presents favorable opportunities for travel and exploration for Sagittarius. The semi-sextile aspect between Uranus in Taurus and the True Node in Aries on January 23rd brings unexpected travel possibilities and the chance to broaden your horizons. Sagittarius individuals may find themselves drawn to spontaneous trips or unique travel experiences during this time.

The conjunction between Venus and Pluto in Capricorn on January 30th further enhances the potential for transformative travel experiences. This alignment may involve trips that bring about personal growth, self-discovery, or a deeper understanding of different cultures and perspectives.

However, it is important for Sagittarius to consider practical aspects such as budget and time constraints before embarking on any travel plans. Planning and preparation are key to making the most of these travel opportunities.

By embracing the spirit of adventure and maintaining a flexible approach, Sagittarius can make the most of the travel opportunities presented in January.

Insight from the stars

The stars advise Sagittarius to focus on self-care, effective communication, and maintaining a sense of balance in all endeavors. By harnessing their natural curiosity, optimism, and adventurous spirit, Sagittarius can seize the opportunities presented in January 2024 and create a fulfilling and successful month.

Best days of the month: January 11th, 12th, 19th, 23rd, 26th, 28th, 30th.

February 2024

Horoscope

February 2024 presents a transformative period for Sagittarius individuals, as the celestial alignments encourage deep introspection, personal growth, and significant changes. This month holds the potential for profound transformations in various aspects of life, urging Sagittarius to embrace the opportunities for self-reflection and advancement.

The conjunction between the Sun and Mercury in Pisces on February 28th signifies a period of heightened intuition and self-awareness for Sagittarius. This alignment fosters deep introspection and encourages individuals to explore their innermost thoughts and emotions. It is a time to gain clarity, make important decisions, and embark on a journey of self-discovery.

Throughout the month, Sagittarius individuals are called to prioritize their emotional well-being and engage in self-care routines. The semi-square aspect between Mars in Aquarius and Neptune in Pisces on February 2nd advises caution regarding excessive physical exertion and the need for rest. Maintaining a balanced lifestyle and listening to the body's needs will be crucial during this period.

Furthermore, the celestial aspects in February inspire Sagittarius to nurture deeper connections in their relationships. The square aspect between Venus in Capricorn and Chiron in Aries on February 5th brings forth the opportunity for emotional healing and growth within partnerships. Honest and open communication will play a vital role in resolving any underlying conflicts or unresolved wounds.

Love

In matters of love, February 2024 encourages Sagittarius individuals to focus on emotional healing and strengthening their connections. The square aspect between Venus in Capricorn and Chiron in Aries on February 5th may bring up past wounds and insecurities, challenging Sagittarius to address them in their relationships. By embracing vulnerability and open communication, Sagittarius can foster deeper emotional intimacy with their partner.

The sextile aspect between Venus in Capricorn and Neptune in Pisces on February 13th enhances romantic experiences and fosters a sense of compassion and understanding. This alignment brings a touch of magic and romance to Sagittarius' love life, allowing for deeper emotional connections and spiritual bonds.

Overall, February invites Sagittarius to focus on self-love, compassion, and nurturing their relationships. By embracing vulnerability, practicing active listening, and fostering a supportive environment, Sagittarius can create a strong foundation for love and cultivate meaningful connections.

Career

Career-wise, February 2024 presents opportunities for professional growth and success for Sagittarius. The conjunction between Mercury and Pluto in Aquarius on February 5th brings transformative energy and heightened mental acuity. This alignment empowers Sagittarius to approach their work with strategic thinking and innovation.

The trine aspect between Venus in Capricorn and Uranus in Taurus on February 7th sparks creativity and the potential for unexpected career advancements. Sagittarius individuals may find themselves exploring new avenues or taking on exciting projects during this period.

However, the square aspect between Mercury in Pisces and Jupiter in Taurus on February 10th may create challenges in terms of communication and decision-making. It is crucial for Sagittarius to remain diligent, seek clarity, and avoid rushing into important career choices during this time.

By harnessing their natural optimism, adaptability, and strategic thinking, Sagittarius can make significant progress in their career endeavors in February.

Finance

Financially, February 2024 calls for caution and practicality for Sagittarius. The semi-square aspect between Venus in Capricorn and Saturn in Pisces on February 10th may introduce some financial restrictions and challenges. It is important for Sagittarius to exercise financial discipline and avoid impulsive spending during this period.

The conjunction between Venus and Mars in Aquarius on February 22nd brings opportunities for financial growth and stability. This alignment encourages Sagittarius to explore new income streams, invest wisely, and consider long-term financial goals.

However, the square aspect between Venus in Aquarius and Jupiter in Taurus on February 24th may create a tendency for overspending or indulgence. It is crucial for Sagittarius to maintain a balanced approach to finances, practice budgeting, and avoid unnecessary risks.

By being mindful of their financial decisions, setting realistic goals, and adopting a disciplined approach, Sagittarius can ensure financial stability and growth in February.

Health

February 2024 highlights the importance of self-care and emotional well-being for Sagittarius. The semi-square aspect between Mars in Aquarius and Neptune in Pisces on February 28th may bring some challenges to physical energy and vitality. It is important for Sagittarius to prioritize rest, relaxation, and self-care practices to maintain a healthy balance.

The sextile aspect between Mercury in Pisces and Chiron in Aries on February 15th supports emotional healing and encourages Sagittarius to address any emotional imbalances or past traumas. This alignment provides an opportunity for self-reflection, therapy, or seeking support from loved ones.

Overall, Sagittarius individuals should focus on maintaining a healthy lifestyle, nurturing their emotional well-being, and incorporating activities that promote relaxation and stress relief. By prioritizing self-care, Sagittarius can navigate any health challenges and foster overall well-being in February.

Travel

February 2024 presents opportunities for travel and exploration for Sagittarius. The sextile aspect between Venus in Aquarius and Mars in Aquarius on February 22nd encourages spontaneous and adventurous travel experiences. Sagittarius individuals may find themselves drawn to unique destinations or engaging in activities that expand their horizons.

However, it is important for Sagittarius to consider practical aspects such as budget and time constraints before making any travel plans. Planning ahead, researching destinations, and being flexible in their itineraries will ensure a smooth and fulfilling travel experience.

By embracing their love for adventure, seeking new experiences, and immersing themselves in different cultures, Sagittarius can make the most of the travel opportunities presented in February.

Insight from the stars

The stars encourage Sagittarius to embrace their intuitive nature, maintain open communication in relationships, and approach their endeavors with patience and mindfulness. By harnessing their natural optimism, adaptability, and strategic thinking,

Sagittarius can navigate challenges and seize the opportunities presented in February.

Best days of the month: February 7th, 13th, 15th, 22nd, 24th, 28th, and 29th.

March 2024

Horoscope

March 2024 brings a dynamic and transformative energy for Sagittarius individuals. This month holds the potential for significant personal growth, emotional healing, and exciting opportunities. The celestial aspects invite Sagittarius to embrace their intuitive nature, explore their emotional depths, and strike a balance between introspection and action.

The conjunction between the Sun and Neptune in Pisces on March 17th amplifies Sagittarius' spiritual and intuitive abilities. This alignment encourages deep introspection, self-reflection, and connection with their inner wisdom. Sagittarius may find themselves drawn to spiritual practices, meditation, or creative endeavors that allow them to tap into their higher consciousness.

Furthermore, the sextile aspect between the Sun in Aries and Jupiter in Taurus on March 1st boosts Sagittarius' optimism and opens doors to growth and expansion. This alignment fuels Sagittarius' adventurous spirit and encourages them to embrace new opportunities with confidence and enthusiasm.

However, it's important for Sagittarius to be mindful of the square aspect between Venus in Pisces and Uranus in Taurus on March 3rd. This alignment cautions against impulsive decision-making or sudden changes in relationships or finances. It is advisable for Sagittarius to approach these areas of life with caution, maintaining stability and considering the long-term implications of their choices.

Overall, March presents a time of self-discovery, spiritual growth, and exciting possibilities for Sagittarius. By embracing their intuitive nature, nurturing their relationships, and remaining grounded in practicality, Sagittarius can make the most of the transformative energy and create a positive impact in various aspects of their life.

Love

In matters of love, March 2024 invites Sagittarius individuals to explore their emotional depths and deepen their connections. The conjunction between Venus and Saturn in Pisces on March 21st brings a sense of stability and commitment in relationships. Sagittarius individuals may experience a deeper level of emotional intimacy and a stronger sense of loyalty.

The semi-sextile aspect between Venus in Pisces and Chiron in Aries on March 26th highlights the importance of healing and addressing any emotional wounds within relationships. This alignment encourages open communication, vulnerability, and mutual support.

Overall, March encourages Sagittarius to prioritize emotional well-being, foster open and honest communication, and embrace the transformative power of love. By nurturing their connections and honoring their emotional needs, Sagittarius can experience deep and meaningful relationships.

Career

Career-wise, March 2024 presents opportunities for growth and expansion for Sagittarius. The sextile aspect between Mercury in Aries and Pluto in Aquarius on March 10th enhances communication and empowers Sagittarius to express their ideas and opinions with confidence. This alignment supports strategic thinking and innovative approaches to work.

The semi-sextile aspect between Mercury in Aries and Saturn in Pisces on March 16th emphasizes the importance of discipline and perseverance in career matters. Sagittarius individuals are encouraged to stay focused and diligent in their pursuits, as this alignment enhances productivity and long-term success.

However, the conjunction between Mercury and Chiron in Aries on March 20th may bring up some insecurities or self-doubt in the career sphere. It is crucial for Sagittarius to address these emotional challenges and seek support when needed.

By embracing their natural curiosity, adaptability, and strategic thinking, Sagittarius can make significant progress in their career endeavors in March.

Finance

Financially, March 2024 calls for caution and practicality for Sagittarius. The square aspect between Venus in Pisces and Uranus in Taurus on March 3rd may introduce some unexpected financial challenges or changes. It is important for Sagittarius to remain adaptable and flexible in their approach to finances during this period.

The sextile aspect between Venus in Pisces and Jupiter in Taurus on March 24th brings opportunities for financial growth and expansion. Sagittarius individuals may encounter favorable financial prospects or receive support from unexpected sources.

However, the semi-square aspect between Venus in Pisces and Pluto in Aquarius on March 25th cautions

Sagittarius to avoid impulsive or excessive spending. It is crucial to maintain a balanced approach, practice budgeting, and make informed financial decisions.

By being mindful of their financial choices, seeking advice when necessary, and maintaining a disciplined approach, Sagittarius can ensure financial stability and growth in March.

Health

March 2024 highlights the importance of maintaining a healthy mind-body balance for Sagittarius. The conjunction between the Sun and Neptune in Pisces on March 17th emphasizes the need for self-care, rest, and relaxation. Sagittarius individuals are encouraged to prioritize their mental and emotional well-being and engage in activities that promote inner peace and tranquility.

The semi-square aspect between the Sun in Aries and Uranus in Taurus on March 25th may bring some restlessness or a need for change in physical routines. It is important for Sagittarius to find a balance between spontaneity and stability, ensuring that they maintain a consistent and healthy lifestyle.

Overall, Sagittarius should focus on self-care, stress management, and maintaining a balanced lifestyle in order to promote optimal health and well-being in March.

Travel

March 2024 presents opportunities for travel and exploration for Sagittarius. The semi-sextile aspect between Mars in Pisces and Neptune in Pisces on March 19th enhances the potential for spiritual and transformative travel experiences. Sagittarius individuals may find themselves drawn to destinations that offer a sense of peace, connection, and self-discovery.

However, it is important for Sagittarius to consider practical aspects such as budget and time constraints before making any travel plans. Planning ahead, researching destinations, and being open to unexpected opportunities will ensure a fulfilling and enriching travel experience.

By embracing their love for adventure, seeking new experiences, and allowing their intuition to guide them, Sagittarius can make the most of the travel opportunities presented in March.

Insight from the stars

This month calls for a balance between intuition and action, emotional healing and vulnerability, and practicality in financial matters.

Best days of the month: March 6th,10th, 17th,20th,21st, 24th and 28th.

April 2024

Horoscope

April is set to be an invigorating and transformative month for Sagittarius individuals. The celestial movements and planetary alignments will have a profound impact on various aspects of your life, urging you to embrace personal growth and seek new opportunities.

The semi-sextile between Mercury in Aries and Venus in Pisces on April 2nd enhances your communication skills and brings a harmonious balance to your relationships. This alignment encourages open and heartfelt conversations, allowing you to express yourself with clarity and compassion. It is an ideal time to resolve conflicts, deepen emotional connections, and strengthen bonds with loved ones.

As the Sun semi-sextiles Saturn in Pisces on April 2nd, you will feel a sense of discipline and responsibility in your actions. This alignment empowers you to overcome challenges and take on additional responsibilities with grace and determination. Your hard work and dedication will be recognized by superiors and colleagues, potentially leading to career advancements or increased professional respect.

Love

In matters of the heart, the conjunction of Venus and Neptune in Pisces on April 3rd creates an enchanting and romantic atmosphere for Sagittarius individuals. This alignment heightens your sensitivity, intuition, and capacity for empathy, allowing you to connect deeply with your partner. It is a time for heartfelt conversations, tender gestures, and shared dreams. Existing relationships will experience a renewed sense of passion and emotional closeness.

For single Sagittarius individuals, the conjunction between Venus and Neptune brings opportunities for a soulful and spiritual connection with a potential partner. You may find yourself drawn to someone who shares your ideals, values, and spiritual outlook, creating a deep and meaningful bond. Trust your instincts and be open to the possibilities that unfold. This alignment also invites you to cultivate self-love and self-acceptance, as it is through honoring your own needs that you will attract a compatible and fulfilling relationship.

Career

April presents a dynamic and proactive period for your professional life, Sagittarius. The Sun's semi-sextile with Saturn in Pisces on April 2nd imbues you with discipline, determination, and a strong work ethic. You will find yourself more focused and committed to your goals, leading to significant progress in your career. This alignment also emphasizes the importance of maintaining a structured approach to your work, managing your time efficiently, and demonstrating reliability.

The semi-square between Mercury in Aries and Mars in Pisces on April 6th indicates a need for careful communication and strategic decision-making. This alignment reminds you to consider the potential impact of your words and actions on others. It is crucial to maintain clarity, avoid impulsivity, and think before you speak. Collaboration and teamwork will be essential during this period, as conflicts may arise if you do not communicate effectively.

Finance

April brings both opportunities and cautionary aspects for your financial situation, Sagittarius. The conjunction of Venus and Pluto in Aries on April 6th suggests the potential for financial growth through investments or joint ventures. However, exercise caution and conduct thorough research before making any significant financial decisions. Seek advice from professionals if needed to ensure that you make informed choices and mitigate risks.

The semi-square between Venus in Aries and Jupiter in Taurus on April 8th advises against impulsive spending and urges you to adopt a balanced approach to finances. While there may be temptations to splurge or indulge in extravagances, it is essential to maintain financial discipline and focus on long-term stability. Review your budget, cut unnecessary expenses, and prioritize saving. Consider seeking expert advice or exploring new investment opportunities that align with your long-term financial goals.

Health

Maintaining your well-being becomes essential during April, Sagittarius. The semi-sextile between Mars in Pisces and Uranus in Taurus on April 3rd encourages you to explore alternative health practices and routines that align with your spiritual and physical needs. Engaging in activities such as yoga, meditation, or energy healing can support your overall well-being and help you find inner balance.

The semi-sextile between Mercury in Aries and Uranus in Taurus on April 13th brings mental stimulation and innovative thinking. It is an excellent time to explore new mental health practices, engage in creative pursuits, or seek out intellectual challenges that promote growth and self-expression. Take time to prioritize self-care and listen to your body's signals. Nurturing your physical well-being through a healthy diet, regular exercise, and sufficient rest will contribute to your overall vitality.

Travel

April presents opportunities for exciting adventures and exploration for Sagittarius individuals. The conjunction between Jupiter and Uranus in Taurus on April 20th sparks a desire for new experiences and expands your horizons. This alignment favors travel that combines adventure, learning, and spiritual enrichment. Whether you embark on a physical journey to a foreign land or immerse yourself in different cultures and belief systems, this is a transformative period for broadening your perspective and embracing new experiences.

Additionally, the semi-sextile between Venus in Aries and Uranus in Taurus on April 22nd further enhances your travel prospects. Unexpected opportunities may arise, allowing you to explore unique destinations or engage in spontaneous getaways. Embrace the spirit of adventure and be open to the possibilities that travel brings. It is through these experiences that you will gain a deeper understanding of yourself and the world around you.

Insight from the stars

Remember to balance your ambitions with self-care and take time to nurture your emotional and physical well-being. This transformative month holds immense potential for growth, fulfillment, and the expansion of your horizons.

Best days of the month: April 4th, 10th, 19th, 20th, 21st, and 24th.

May 2024

Horoscope

May brings a dynamic and transformative energy for Sagittarius individuals. The celestial movements and planetary alignments will have a profound impact on various aspects of your life, urging you to embrace change, seek new experiences, and deepen your connections with others.

The square between Venus in Taurus and Pluto in Aquarius on May 1st creates a transformative energy in your relationships and financial matters. This alignment brings intensity and depth to your love life, as well as the potential for financial transformations. It is a time to reassess your values, let go of unhealthy patterns, and establish a stronger sense of self-worth.

As Mars in Aries sextiles Pluto in Aquarius on May 3rd, you will feel a surge of energy and determination in pursuing your goals. This alignment empowers you to take charge of your life and make bold moves in your career or personal endeavors. It is a favorable time for strategic planning and taking calculated risks that can lead to long-term success.

Love

In matters of the heart, May brings a mix of passion, growth, and healing for Sagittarius. The conjunction between Venus and Jupiter in Taurus on May 23rd creates an atmosphere of love, joy, and expansion in your relationships. This alignment brings positive energy, harmony, and an increased desire for commitment. Existing relationships will thrive as you and your partner experience deep emotional connection and shared aspirations.

For single Sagittarius individuals, this alignment signals the potential for a significant romantic encounter or a deepening of a connection with someone special. You may attract a partner who shares your values, vision, and spiritual beliefs. Embrace the opportunities for love and be open to the possibilities that present themselves.

Career

May presents a transformative and powerful period for your professional life, Sagittarius. The conjunction between the Sun and Jupiter in Taurus on May 18th brings expansion, abundance, and opportunities for growth in your career. This alignment opens doors to new ventures, promotions, or recognition for your hard work. It is a time to take bold steps, pursue your ambitions, and showcase your skills and talents.

The semi-sextile between Mars in Aries and Saturn in Pisces on May 24th encourages you to find a balance between assertiveness and discipline in your work. This alignment supports you in taking a practical and strategic approach to your career goals. It is important to be patient, work diligently, and remain focused on long-term success. Your dedication and perseverance will lead to significant achievements.

Finance

May brings a mix of opportunities and challenges in your financial matters, Sagittarius. The semi-square between Venus in Taurus and Neptune in Pisces on May 10th warns against impulsive spending or hasty financial decisions. It is essential to exercise caution, review your budget, and seek expert advice before making significant investments or commitments.

The trine between Venus in Gemini and Pluto in Aquarius on May 25th offers the potential for financial gains through strategic partnerships or joint ventures. This alignment encourages you to explore innovative approaches and collaborations that align with your long-term financial goals. Remain vigilant and focused on maintaining financial stability while pursuing growth opportunities.

Health

Maintaining your well-being becomes essential during May, Sagittarius. The semi-sextile between the Sun in Gemini and Chiron in Aries on May 27th brings a heightened awareness of your physical and emotional health. This alignment encourages you to address any lingering health issues or emotional wounds. Seek holistic healing approaches, engage in self-care practices, and prioritize self-compassion and self-acceptance.

The conjunction between Mars and Chiron in Aries on May 29th emphasizes the importance of taking care of your physical and mental well-being. Listen to your body's signals, rest when needed, and seek support if you experience any health challenges. This alignment also invites you to engage in activities that bring you joy, inspiration, and spiritual nourishment.

Travel

May presents opportunities for transformative travel experiences and exploration for Sagittarius individuals. The conjunction between the Sun and Uranus in Taurus on May 13th sparks a desire for adventure, freedom, and breaking out of your comfort zone. This alignment encourages you to embark on spontaneous trips, explore new cultures, and embrace unfamiliar experiences that expand your horizons.

The sextile between Venus in Taurus and Saturn in Pisces on May 13th favors travel plans that combine relaxation, spiritual growth, and cultural immersion. It is a favorable time to connect with different perspectives, engage in meaningful conversations, and deepen your understanding of the world.

Insights from the stars

It is essential to approach challenges with patience, caution, and a strategic mindset. Balance your personal and professional aspirations with self-care and mindful decision-making. The stars support you in aligning your actions with your long-term goals and living a life that is true to your authentic self.

Best days of the month: May 13th, 18th, 23rd, 25th, 27th, 29th, and 31st.

June 2024

Horoscope

June 2024 holds immense potential for growth and transformation in various aspects of your life, dear Sagittarius. With the semi-sextile between Mars in Aries and Uranus in Taurus on June 1st, you'll feel a surge of motivation and determination. This alignment ignites your adventurous spirit and prompts you to embrace new experiences. Trust your instincts and seize the opportunities that come your way, as they may lead to exciting developments and significant personal growth.

The quintile aspect between the Sun and Neptune on June 1st enhances your intuition and creativity. Your imagination will be heightened, making it an ideal time for artistic pursuits or spiritual exploration. Use this cosmic influence to connect with your inner wisdom and tap into your deepest aspirations.

Love

In matters of the heart, June brings promising energy for Sagittarius. The sextile between the Sun and the True Node on June 3rd fosters harmony and understanding in your relationships. This alignment encourages open and honest communication, enabling you to deepen your connections with your partner. If you're single, this aspect brings the potential for meeting someone who shares your values and aspirations for the future.

On June 4th, Venus and the True Node form a sextile, intensifying the potential for soulful connections and romantic encounters. The conjunction between the Sun and Venus on the same day amplifies the energy of love and harmony, making it an ideal time for romantic gestures and nurturing existing bonds. Whether in a committed relationship or seeking love, June presents an opportunity to cultivate meaningful connections and experience heartfelt moments of joy.

Career

Career-wise, June holds the promise of growth and success for Sagittarius. The trine aspect between

61

Jupiter in Gemini and Pluto in Aquarius on June 2nd empowers you to embrace change and achieve success through strategic planning. This alignment favors collaboration and networking, urging you to connect with others in your professional field. By building alliances and exploring new avenues, you can open doors to exciting opportunities and advancement.

However, the semi-square between Mars and Saturn on June 14th reminds you to exercise patience and perseverance in your career endeavors. Challenges may arise, but with determination and a disciplined approach, you can overcome them. Stay focused on your long-term ambitions, and don't let setbacks discourage you. Remember that each obstacle is an opportunity for growth and learning.

Finance

Financially, June presents a mix of opportunities and challenges. The quintile aspect between Mercury and Neptune on June 8th enhances your financial intuition, allowing you to make wise decisions and investments. Trust your gut instincts, but also seek advice from trusted professionals if needed. This alignment favors creative financial endeavors, such as investing in artistic ventures or exploring new income streams.

However, the square aspect between Venus and Saturn on June 8th may introduce some financial constraints, requiring you to budget and be mindful of your expenses. This is not a time for impulsive purchases or risky financial decisions. Instead, focus on long-term financial stability and consider implementing a savings plan. By maintaining a balanced and responsible approach, you can navigate any challenges and build a solid foundation for your future.

Health

In terms of health and well-being, June encourages Sagittarius to prioritize self-care and holistic wellness. The semi-square between Mercury and Chiron on June 6th reminds you to pay attention to your mental and emotional health. Take time to reflect, process your emotions, and seek support if needed. Engaging in activities that bring you joy and practicing mindfulness will contribute to your overall well-being.

June also presents opportunities for physical activity and rejuvenation. The semi-sextile between Mars and Jupiter on June 15th fuels your energy levels and inspires you to engage in regular exercise. Whether it's outdoor activities, gym workouts, or yoga sessions, prioritize movement and physical vitality. Balancing work and rest is crucial, so make sure to incorporate moments of relaxation and rejuvenation into your routine.

Travel

Travel-wise, June offers Sagittarius the chance to explore new horizons and broaden their perspectives. The semi-square between Mercury and Uranus on June 22nd sparks a desire for adventure and spontaneity. Embrace this cosmic energy by planning a trip to a destination that captivates your imagination. Whether it's a solo adventure or a group excursion, traveling in June can provide a refreshing change of scenery and deepen your appreciation for different cultures.

The semi-sextile between Venus and Jupiter on June 22nd enhances the enjoyment of travel and encourages you to seek new experiences. Embrace the sense of discovery and be open to unexpected encounters and opportunities during your journeys. Engage with the local culture, try new cuisines, and immerse yourself in the beauty of your surroundings. Traveling in June holds the potential for transformative experiences and unforgettable memories.

Insight from the stars

Embrace the opportunities that come your way, trust in your abilities, and stay true to your values. With dedication, perseverance, and a willingness to embrace change, you will navigate the month with grace and make significant progress towards your goals.

Best days of the month: June 3rd, 8th, 13th, 15th, 19th, 24th and 29th.

July 2024

Horoscope

In July 2024, Sagittarius, you will experience a mix of energetic and transformative influences. The month kicks off with Jupiter in Gemini semi-square Chiron in Aries, encouraging you to address any emotional wounds or insecurities that may hinder your personal growth. This aspect invites you to explore your beliefs and expand your knowledge, as Mercury quintiles Mars, boosting your mental agility and drive for self-expression.

The Sun in Cancer semi-squares Uranus in Taurus, urging you to embrace change and break free from any restrictions. Meanwhile, Mercury trine Neptune enhances your intuitive abilities, making it an excellent time for introspection and spiritual pursuits. Be cautious, however, as the Sun squares the True Node in Aries, indicating potential conflicts between your personal desires and your sense of duty.

Venus trine Saturn provides stability and support in your relationships, fostering deep connections and commitment. However, be wary of Mercury's opposition to Pluto, which may lead to power struggles or intense communication challenges. Uranus' semi-square with the True Node suggests a need for balance between your individuality and your role within your social circle.

Love

In matters of the heart, July 2024 brings opportunities for growth and transformation for Sagittarius. With Venus in Cancer, you will experience a deep emotional connection with your partner or potential love interests. The trine to Saturn encourages stability and commitment, making it a favorable time for long-term relationships. You may feel inclined to deepen the bond and create a sense of security.

However, challenges may arise as Venus squares Chiron, highlighting potential insecurities or past wounds that need healing. This aspect calls for open and honest communication with your partner to overcome any emotional barriers. It is crucial to address any unresolved issues and work together towards healing and understanding.

For single Sagittarius individuals, the trine between Venus and Saturn may attract someone who appreciates your sincerity and loyalty. Be open to forming connections and allowing yourself to be vulnerable. However, with the opposition between

Venus and Pluto, it is essential to maintain healthy boundaries and not let power dynamics or possessiveness affect your relationships.

Career

July 2024 presents both challenges and opportunities in your career, Sagittarius. With Mercury in Leo, your communication skills are heightened, making it an ideal time to express your ideas and take the lead in projects. The sextile between Mercury and Jupiter enhances your persuasive abilities, allowing you to effectively influence others and expand your professional network.

However, the square aspect between Mercury and Uranus can bring unexpected changes or conflicts within your work environment. It is important to adapt quickly to new situations and remain flexible in your approach. Embracing innovative ideas and taking calculated risks can lead to breakthroughs and career advancements.

The opposition between Mercury and Pluto indicates power struggles or intense negotiations. Be cautious in your interactions with colleagues or superiors, and ensure that your communication remains respectful and diplomatic. It may also be beneficial to seek constructive feedback and engage in self-reflection to enhance your professional growth.

Finance

Financially, July 2024 presents a mixed bag for Sagittarius. The trine between Venus and Saturn brings stability and discipline to your financial matters. It is an excellent time for budgeting, long-term planning, and making wise investments. Your practical approach and attention to detail will contribute to financial security and prosperity.

However, with the square aspect between Venus and Chiron, there may be emotional factors influencing your spending habits. Be mindful of any impulsive or comfort-driven purchases that may arise as a result of unresolved emotional issues. Focus on finding healthier ways to address emotional needs that do not involve overspending or indulgence.

The semi-square between the Sun and Uranus suggests the potential for unexpected expenses or sudden changes in your financial situation. It is crucial to have a contingency plan in place and maintain a flexible approach to adapt to any financial fluctuations that may arise.

Taking the time to review your financial goals and seek professional advice can help you make informed decisions and ensure long-term stability. Consider exploring alternative sources of income or investment opportunities that align with your values and long-term aspirations

Health

In terms of health and well-being, July 2024 urges Sagittarius to prioritize self-care and emotional well-being. The semi-square between the Sun and Uranus may bring sudden energy fluctuations or disruptions to your routines. Pay attention to your body's signals and adapt your activities accordingly to maintain a healthy balance.

With Mercury in Leo, it is essential to pay attention to your mental health. Engage in activities that promote self-expression and creativity, as these can have a positive impact on your overall well-being. Regular meditation or mindfulness practices can also help you stay grounded and alleviate stress.

The opposition between Mercury and Pluto suggests the need to address any deep-seated emotional issues that may be affecting your mental and physical health. Consider seeking support from a therapist or engaging in introspective practices to release emotional burdens and promote healing.

Maintaining a balanced lifestyle is key during this period. Make time for regular exercise, nutritious meals, and sufficient rest. The trine between Venus and Saturn encourages self-discipline and self-care practices that support your overall vitality.

Travel

In July 2024, Sagittarius, you may experience opportunities for exciting travel or exploration. The trine between Venus and Saturn indicates a favorable time for planning trips that offer both relaxation and cultural enrichment. Consider destinations that align with your interests and allow you to expand your knowledge and perspective.

The square aspect between Mercury and Uranus suggests the potential for spontaneous or last-minute travel plans. Stay open to unexpected opportunities that may arise and be prepared to adapt your itineraries or schedules accordingly. This can lead to exciting adventures and memorable experiences.

However, it is important to maintain a balance between exploration and self-care. The semi-square between the Sun and Uranus may disrupt your routines, potentially leading to fatigue or burnout. Make sure to incorporate rest periods and self-care activities into your travel plans to avoid exhaustion.

Consider engaging in mindful travel practices that allow you to connect with your surroundings on a deeper level. Embrace new cultures, try local cuisine, and engage with the local community to enhance your travel experiences.

Insight from the stars

You are encouraged to explore new knowledge, expand your horizons, and address any emotional wounds that may hinder your progress.

Best days of the month: July 2nd, 9th, 10th, 18th, 19th, 21st, and 31st.

August 2024

Horoscope

In August 2024, Sagittarius, you will experience a dynamic and transformative month that encourages personal growth and self-discovery. The month begins with Mars sextile the True Node, highlighting opportunities for growth and positive changes in your life path. However, the semi-square between Mars and Chiron suggests that you may need to confront and heal any deep-seated wounds or insecurities that could hinder your progress.

Venus quintile Jupiter infuses your relationships and social interactions with harmony and positivity. It is a time for joy and celebration, and you may find yourself surrounded by supportive and like-minded individuals. However, be cautious of the square aspect between Venus and Uranus, as it may introduce unexpected disruptions or changes in your romantic life or social circle. Maintain flexibility and adaptability in your relationships to navigate any challenges that may arise.

The Sun's biquintile with Saturn emphasizes the importance of balance and responsibility in your daily life. It encourages you to find a harmonious rhythm between work and play, ensuring that you prioritize your obligations while still making time for self-care and personal enjoyment.

Love

August 2024 brings both passion and challenges to your love life, Sagittarius. With Venus in Leo, your romantic pursuits are infused with warmth, charisma, and a desire for deep connections. You radiate confidence and attract potential partners who appreciate your authentic self-expression.

The quintile between Venus and Jupiter enhances your romantic experiences, promoting joy, adventure, and a sense of expansiveness in your relationships. This aspect encourages you to embrace new experiences and open yourself up to love without fear or reservations.

However, the square aspect between Venus and Uranus may introduce unexpected twists and turns in your romantic life. Sudden changes or unconventional attractions could challenge your existing relationship dynamics or push you out of your comfort zone. It is crucial to maintain open and honest communication with your partner, embracing flexibility and adaptability to navigate any unexpected shifts.

For single Sagittarius individuals, this period may bring exciting and unconventional romantic prospects. Be open to new connections and take a chance on love, even if it deviates from your usual expectations or patterns.

Career

August 2024 presents both challenges and opportunities in your career, Sagittarius. With Mars in Gemini, you possess a sharp intellect and persuasive communication skills that can propel you forward in your professional pursuits. The conjunction between Mars and Jupiter further amplifies your ambition and drive, opening doors for expansion and success.

However, the square aspect between Mars and Saturn indicates potential obstacles or conflicts within your work environment. You may encounter resistance or face limitations in achieving your goals. Patience and perseverance will be key during this period, as you may need to demonstrate your dedication and willingness to overcome challenges.

It is crucial to maintain a diplomatic approach in your professional interactions, as the sesquiquadrate between Mercury and Venus may bring communication challenges or power struggles. Be mindful of your words and seek common ground to foster harmonious relationships with colleagues and superiors.

Finance

Financially, August 2024 calls for careful planning and a pragmatic approach for Sagittarius. The Sun's quincunx with Saturn reminds you to find a balance between your financial obligations and your desire for personal enjoyment. Avoid impulsive spending and focus on long-term financial stability.

The biquintile between Venus and Pluto suggests potential financial gains through strategic investments or collaborations. It is a favorable time to seek advice from financial experts or explore innovative approaches to grow your wealth. However, exercise caution and thoroughly research any financial opportunities before committing.

The opposition between Venus and Neptune cautions against unrealistic financial expectations or potential scams. Be discerning and trust your instincts when making financial decisions. Seek clarity and avoid making major financial commitments without thorough consideration.

Consider revisiting your budget and financial goals during this period. Implement practical strategies, such as saving and budgeting, to ensure financial security. Remember to strike a balance between enjoying your resources and planning for the future.

Health

In terms of health and well-being, August 2024 encourages Sagittarius to prioritize self-care and emotional balance. The Sun's sesquiquadrate with Chiron may bring up past wounds or emotional challenges that require healing. Take the time to address any underlying emotional issues and seek support from trusted individuals or professionals.

The biquintile between Mercury and Neptune enhances your intuition and spiritual well-being. Engage in practices such as meditation, yoga, or journaling to promote mental clarity and emotional equilibrium. Listen to your body's needs and prioritize self-care routines that nurture your overall well-being.

The square aspect between Mars and Saturn may introduce potential physical challenges or limitations. Practice moderation in physical activities and avoid pushing yourself beyond your limits. Incorporate rest and recovery periods into your routine to maintain a healthy balance between activity and relaxation.

Maintaining a balanced diet is essential during this period. Focus on nourishing your body with nutritious foods and staying hydrated. Consider incorporating stress-reducing practices, such as mindfulness or gentle exercise, to promote overall vitality.

Travel

August 2024 presents opportunities for travel and exploration for Sagittarius. With Venus in Virgo, you may find pleasure and fulfillment in planning and organizing your travel experiences. Attention to detail and practicality will contribute to smooth and enjoyable trips.

The sesquiquadrate between Venus and Chiron suggests the need for emotional healing during your travels. It may be beneficial to engage in self-reflection and address any emotional triggers that arise while exploring new environments. Be open to experiencing different cultures and perspectives, as this can deepen your personal growth and broaden your horizons.

The biquintile between Mercury and Neptune enhances your sense of adventure and curiosity. Embrace spontaneity and be open to unexpected detours or changes in your travel plans. Allow yourself to connect with the spiritual and mystical aspects of the places you visit.

Maintain flexibility and adaptability in your travel itineraries, as the opposition between Venus and Jupiter may introduce unexpected shifts or changes.

Embrace these opportunities as chances for growth and new experiences.

Insight from the stars

Allow your intuition to guide you as you explore new horizons and embark on exciting journeys. Trust in your inner strength and embrace the transformative power of the stars.

Best days of the month: August 7th, 15th, 22nd, 23rd, 26th, 28th and 31st.

September 2024

Horoscope

September 2024 brings a blend of intense energies and transformative opportunities for Sagittarius. This month, you will be guided to delve deep within yourself, confronting emotional wounds and embracing personal growth. The presence of Mercury in Leo encourages heartfelt communication and self-expression, while the trine aspect between Mercury and Chiron supports healing and self-discovery.

The Sun's quintile with Mars infuses you with a dynamic and courageous spirit, empowering you to take bold actions and pursue your passions. However, be mindful of the square between Mars and Neptune, as it may introduce some confusion or deception in your pursuits. Trust your instincts and maintain clarity to avoid unnecessary pitfalls.

In the realm of relationships, Venus's opposition with the True Node signifies a period of soul-searching and self-reflection. You may find yourself reevaluating your desires and seeking alignment with your true path. It is essential to strike a balance between your personal needs and the needs of your partner or loved ones. Open and honest communication is key to maintaining harmony and finding common ground.

Love

September 2024 brings a profound exploration of love and relationships for Sagittarius. With Venus in Libra, you seek balance and harmony in your romantic connections. The quincunx aspect between Venus and Saturn encourages you to reevaluate your commitments and find equilibrium between personal freedom and partnership.

The sesquiquadrate between Venus and Jupiter may introduce some tension and conflicting desires in your love life. It is important to strike a balance between adventure and stability, ensuring that you honor your personal growth while nurturing your relationships.

For single Sagittarius individuals, this period encourages self-reflection and exploration of your true desires. Trust your intuition and take the time to understand what you truly seek in a partner. Embrace opportunities for growth and expand your social circle to meet like-minded individuals who align with your values and aspirations.

Career

September 2024 presents both challenges and growth opportunities in your career, Sagittarius. With the Sun's opposition to Saturn, you may face obstacles or limitations in achieving your professional goals. Patience, perseverance, and a strategic approach are essential during this period. Focus on building a solid foundation and demonstrate your commitment and dedication to your work.

The trine aspect between Mercury and Uranus enhances your innovative and creative thinking, allowing you to find unique solutions to challenges in your professional life. Embrace new technologies or approaches that can streamline your work processes and increase efficiency.

Collaboration and effective communication play a crucial role in your career development. The sesquiquadrate between Mercury and Neptune reminds you to maintain clarity and avoid misunderstandings in your professional interactions. Be proactive in seeking clarity and ensure that your intentions and ideas are effectively communicated to avoid any miscommunication.

Finance

Financially, September 2024 calls for careful planning and practicality for Sagittarius. The trine aspect between Venus and Jupiter suggests potential financial gains through strategic investments or collaborations. It is a favorable time to seek advice from financial experts or explore new avenues for wealth growth. However, be cautious of overspending or impulsive financial decisions, as the opposition between Venus and Chiron may create emotional triggers or vulnerabilities in your relationship with money.

The sesquiquadrate between Venus and Saturn reminds you to prioritize financial stability and long-term planning. Develop a budgeting strategy and assess your financial commitments to ensure a secure and balanced approach to your resources. Seek opportunities for professional development or additional sources of income to enhance your financial standing.

Health

In terms of health and well-being, September 2024 urges Sagittarius to prioritize self-care and emotional well-being. The trine aspect between the Sun and Pluto encourages deep inner transformation and healing. Take the time to explore any emotional wounds or patterns that may be affecting your physical and mental health. Engage in practices such as therapy, meditation, or journaling to support your healing journey.

The opposition between Mercury and Neptune may introduce some mental fog or confusion. Prioritize mental clarity by implementing stress-reducing techniques, such as mindfulness or gentle exercise. Ensure that you are getting enough rest and relaxation to maintain your overall vitality.

Maintaining a balanced diet and regular exercise routine is crucial during this period. Focus on nourishing your body with nutritious foods and staying hydrated. Incorporate physical activities that bring you joy and help release any pent-up energy or stress.

Travel

September 2024 presents opportunities for travel and exploration for Sagittarius. With Venus in Libra, you seek beauty, harmony, and cultural experiences during your journeys. Embrace opportunities to connect with diverse cultures, expand your horizons, and deepen your understanding of the world.

The quincunx aspect between Venus and Uranus encourages flexibility and adaptability in your travel plans. Embrace unexpected detours or changes in your itinerary, as they may lead to unique and enriching experiences. Be open to spontaneity and immerse yourself fully in the local customs and traditions.

The trine between Venus and Jupiter enhances your social interactions during travel. Embrace opportunities to connect with like-minded individuals, build new friendships, and create lasting memories. Engage in activities that allow you to immerse yourself in the local culture, such as trying new cuisines or exploring historical sites.

Insight from the stars

Remember, the universe is conspiring in your favor, encouraging you to embrace your authenticity, seize every opportunity, and ignite the world with your vibrant spirit.

Best days of the month: September 2nd, 10th, 15th, 19th, 22nd, 26th, 30th.

October 2024

Horoscope

In October 2024, Sagittarius, you can expect a month filled with opportunities for personal growth and development. The planetary aspects indicate that you may experience a significant shift in various areas of your life, urging you to embrace change and explore new possibilities.

This month, your adventurous and optimistic nature will be amplified, pushing you to step outside of your comfort zone and pursue exciting endeavors. The influence of Mercury in Libra encourages you to communicate your ideas and opinions with clarity and diplomacy, enabling you to form harmonious connections with others. It's a favorable time to engage in negotiations or collaborative projects that can lead to mutual benefits.

In summary, October 2024 brings exciting prospects for Sagittarius. Embrace change, nurture your relationships, focus on long-term financial stability, prioritize self-care, and seize travel opportunities. By doing so, you'll make the most of the transformative energy surrounding you this month.

Love

Sagittarius, get ready for a passionate and transformative month in love during October 2024. The planetary aspects indicate that your relationships will undergo significant changes, bringing both intense emotions and profound growth.

Venus, the planet of love and desire, transiting through Scorpio, heightens your romantic inclinations. You'll experience a surge of intensity in your partnerships, and emotional connections will deepen. It's a powerful time for bonding and intimacy, allowing you to explore the depths of your emotions and connect with your partner on a soul level.

Communication will play a crucial role in your relationships this month. Mercury's influence in Libra enhances your ability to express your thoughts and emotions with clarity and diplomacy. Take this opportunity to engage in open and honest conversations with your partner. Discuss your desires, fears, and aspirations, as this will foster deeper understanding and strengthen the foundation of your relationship.

For single Sagittarians, October brings the potential for passionate encounters and transformative connections. You may find yourself drawn to individuals who stimulate your mind and challenge your perspectives. Embrace these connections, but ensure that they align with your values and long-term goals.

However, with the presence of Saturn in Pisces, you may experience occasional challenges in your love life. Saturn's influence can bring forth issues related to commitment or emotional boundaries. It's important to communicate openly and honestly with your partner, addressing any concerns or insecurities that may arise.

Career

Sagittarius, October 2024 presents exciting opportunities for professional growth and advancement. The planetary aspects indicate that your career will flourish as you harness your intellectual abilities, communication skills, and natural optimism.

Jupiter's influence in Gemini brings forth a heightened intellectual curiosity and a thirst for knowledge. This is an ideal time for networking, attending seminars or workshops, and pursuing further education. Your enthusiasm and willingness to learn will attract the attention of superiors and colleagues, opening doors for new opportunities and collaborations.

Mercury's presence in Libra enhances your communication skills, making it easier for you to express your ideas, negotiate contracts, or engage in persuasive presentations. Use this skill to your advantage by taking the lead in discussions and sharing your unique insights. Your eloquence and diplomatic approach will impress others and contribute to your professional success.

However, it's important to remain focused and organized during this period of growth. Saturn's presence in Pisces reminds you to pay attention to detail, adhere to deadlines, and maintain a disciplined work ethic. By demonstrating reliability and responsibility, you'll earn the trust and respect of your superiors, potentially leading to promotions or increased responsibilities.

Collaborations and partnerships may also play a significant role in your career during October. Look for opportunities to join forces with like-minded individuals or participate in group projects. Working in a team environment will foster creativity, broaden your perspectives, and help you achieve your goals more efficiently.

Finance

Sagittarius, October 2024 brings a need for responsible financial management and cautious decision-making. The planetary aspects indicate that while there are opportunities for financial gains, it's important to approach your finances with a strategic mindset and a long-term perspective.

Saturn's presence in Pisces reminds you to be disciplined and practical when it comes to your financial choices. Avoid impulsive spending and prioritize your financial stability and security. It may be wise to consult a financial advisor or create a budget that aligns with your long-term goals. By adopting a cautious approach, you can safeguard your financial well-being and establish a solid foundation for the future.

Venus's trine with Saturn suggests that strategic investments and collaborations can bring financial rewards. If you have been considering entering into partnerships or exploring investment opportunities, now may be an auspicious time to do so. However, conduct thorough research and carefully assess the risks before making any financial commitments.

Additionally, focus on enhancing your financial literacy during October. Educate yourself about investment strategies, savings plans, and money management. Taking a proactive approach to your financial well-being will empower you to make informed decisions and take advantage of favorable opportunities when they arise.

While financial stability is crucial, don't let it overshadow your enjoyment of life. Allow yourself to indulge in small pleasures and experiences that bring you joy, but do so within the boundaries of your budget.

Remember to set aside funds for unexpected expenses or emergencies. Building a financial safety net will provide peace of mind and protect you from financial stress in the long run.

Health

Sagittarius, October 2024 highlights the importance of prioritizing your health and well-being. The planetary aspects indicate that maintaining a balance between physical and emotional wellness is essential for your overall vitality and happiness.

With Mars transiting through Cancer, your energy levels may fluctuate, and emotions may impact your physical well-being. It's crucial to find healthy outlets for your emotions and channel your energy positively. Engage in regular physical activities that bring you joy and help you release any pent-up emotions. Yoga, swimming, or outdoor exercises can be particularly beneficial for your mind and body during this time.

Emotional well-being plays a significant role in your overall health. Take time to reflect on your feelings, and if necessary, seek the support of a therapist or counselor. Expressing your emotions in a healthy way will prevent them from manifesting as physical symptoms or stress-related ailments.

Maintaining a balanced diet is key to supporting your energy levels and immune system. Focus on incorporating nourishing foods into your meals, such as fresh fruits and vegetables, lean proteins, and whole grains. Stay hydrated and avoid excessive consumption of processed or sugary foods.

Ensure that you allocate sufficient time for rest and rejuvenation. Quality sleep is vital for your overall well-being and can significantly impact your energy levels and cognitive function. Establish a relaxing bedtime routine, create a peaceful sleep environment, and aim for a consistent sleep schedule.

During October, it's essential to listen to your body's signals and address any health concerns promptly. Don't ignore symptoms or postpone medical appointments. Proactive care and timely intervention will support your overall health and prevent potential complications.

Practice self-care rituals that nourish your mind, body, and soul. Engage in activities that bring you joy, whether it's spending time in nature, practicing mindfulness, or pursuing hobbies that ignite your passion. Taking care of yourself holistically will contribute to your overall happiness and well-being.

Travel

Sagittarius, October 2024 presents exciting opportunities for travel and exploration. The planetary aspects indicate that your adventurous spirit and desire for new experiences will be heightened, making this month an ideal time to embark on journeys that broaden your horizons.

Whether it's a short weekend getaway or a longer international trip, embrace the spirit of adventure and explore new destinations. Traveling during this period will provide you with inspiration, expand your cultural knowledge, and allow you to connect with like-minded individuals.

Consider visiting places that offer opportunities for spiritual growth or personal development. Retreats, workshops, or immersive cultural experiences can have a profound impact on your journey of self-discovery. Engaging with different cultures and perspectives will broaden your understanding of the world and foster personal growth.

While traveling, be open to unexpected encounters and serendipitous experiences. Embrace spontaneity and allow yourself to be fully present in each moment. Keep a travel journal to capture your thoughts, feelings, and memorable experiences, as it will serve as a cherished memento of your journey.

Practical preparations are essential for smooth travels. Research your destination, familiarize yourself with local customs and traditions, and ensure that you have the necessary travel documents. Take appropriate safety precautions and stay informed about any travel advisories or restrictions.

If international travel is not feasible, consider exploring local attractions and hidden gems in your own region. Often, there are hidden treasures waiting to be discovered close to home. Engaging in local adventures can be equally enriching and provide a fresh perspective on your surroundings.

Remember to prioritize self-care while traveling. Take breaks when needed, stay hydrated, and prioritize restful sleep. Engaging in physical activities, such as hiking or yoga, can help you stay energized and balanced throughout your journey.

Insight from the stars

The stars advise you, Sagittarius, to embrace change and step outside your comfort zone.

Best days of the month: October 4th, 8th, 12th, 14th, 22nd, 28th, and 31st

November 2024

Horoscope

November brings a vibrant and adventurous energy to Sagittarius individuals. With Jupiter, their ruling planet, in Gemini, there is a harmonious sextile aspect with Chiron in Aries on November 2. This alignment encourages Sagittarians to embrace their natural curiosity and explore new horizons. It's an ideal time to expand their knowledge, engage in meaningful conversations, and connect with like-minded individuals.

Additionally, on November 2, Mercury in Scorpio forms a beneficial trine aspect with Mars in Cancer, boosting Sagittarians' mental agility and communication skills. This alignment enhances their ability to express their ideas with precision and passion, making them persuasive communicators.

Furthermore, the sextile between Mercury in Scorpio and Pluto in Capricorn on November 2 empowers Sagittarius individuals to delve into deep, transformative conversations. They have the opportunity to uncover hidden truths and gain profound insights into themselves and others.

Love

In matters of love, Sagittarians will experience a mix of excitement and challenges in November. On November 3, Venus in Sagittarius opposes Jupiter in Gemini, creating a passionate and intense energy. Sagittarians may feel a strong attraction towards someone but must be cautious not to let their enthusiasm blind them to potential red flags. It's important to balance their desire for adventure with a grounded perspective.

The trine aspect between Venus in Sagittarius and Chiron in Aries on the same day brings healing and growth to Sagittarians' relationships. They have the opportunity to address old wounds and foster deeper emotional connections. Single Sagittarians may find themselves drawn to individuals who embody qualities they seek in a partner, and it could lead to a meaningful and transformative bond.

Career

Career-wise, Sagittarius individuals are in for a dynamic and productive month in November. The sesquiquadrate aspect between the Sun in Scorpio and Neptune in Pisces on November 4 emphasizes the importance of maintaining a clear vision and avoiding distractions. Sagittarians should trust their intuition while staying grounded in reality to achieve their professional goals successfully.

The trine aspect between the Sun in Scorpio and Saturn in Pisces on November 4 brings stability and discipline to Sagittarians' endeavors. They can excel in areas that require structure and long-term planning. It's an opportune time to take on new responsibilities, showcase their leadership skills, and gain recognition from superiors.

Additionally, the opposition between Mercury in Sagittarius and Jupiter in Gemini on November 18 encourages Sagittarians to think big and embrace their natural intellectual prowess. They may find themselves in situations where their ideas and opinions are highly valued, leading to exciting collaborations and professional growth.

Finance

Sagittarius individuals will experience a generally positive financial outlook in November. The quincunx aspect between Venus in Sagittarius and Uranus in Taurus on November 7 reminds them to maintain a balance between their desire for spontaneity and the need for financial stability. It's important for Sagittarians to avoid impulsive spending and instead focus on long-term financial goals.

The square aspect between Venus in Sagittarius and Neptune in Pisces on November 9 highlights the importance of clarity and discernment when it comes to financial matters. Sagittarians should be cautious about potential illusions or unrealistic investment opportunities. Seeking expert advice or conducting thorough research can help them make informed decisions.

Health

Sagittarius individuals should prioritize their physical and mental well-being in November. The opposition between Mars in Cancer and Pluto in Capricorn on November 3 may create moments of intensity and emotional upheaval. It is essential for Sagittarians to find healthy outlets for their emotions, such as engaging in regular exercise, practicing mindfulness, or seeking support from loved ones.

The sesquiquadrate aspect between the Sun in Scorpio and Chiron in Aries on November 26 encourages Sagittarians to focus on self-care and healing. They may need to address any lingering

YOUR COMPLETE SAGITTARIUS 2024 PERSONAL HOROSCOPE

physical or emotional wounds to maintain their overall well-being. Engaging in activities that bring joy, such as spending time in nature or pursuing creative hobbies, can provide a much-needed sense of balance.

Travel

November presents exciting opportunities for travel and exploration for Sagittarius individuals. With Jupiter in Gemini sextile Chiron in Aries on November 2, Sagittarians are encouraged to embrace their adventurous spirit and expand their horizons. Whether it's a short weekend getaway or a longer international trip, this is an ideal time to satisfy their wanderlust and gain new cultural experiences.

The biquintile aspect between the Sun and True Node on November 3 further enhances Sagittarians' travel prospects. They may find themselves at the right place and the right time, encountering serendipitous moments and meeting inspiring individuals along the way. Sagittarians should remain open to spontaneous detours and unexpected opportunities that may arise during their travels.

Insight from the stars

In November, Sagittarius individuals are advised to balance their enthusiasm for new experiences with a grounded approach. While it's important to embrace adventure and exploration, they should also exercise caution and discernment in all matters.

Best days of the month: November 2nd, 3rd, 4th, 9th, 18th, 26th and 30th.

December 2024

Horoscope

December brings a transformative energy to Sagittarius individuals, encouraging them to reflect, grow, and embrace new possibilities. The biquintile aspect between Venus and Jupiter on December 1 ignites a sense of optimism and expansion in Sagittarians' lives. This planetary alignment enhances their social interactions and brings joyful and harmonious experiences.

On December 2, Mercury in Sagittarius forms a beneficial trine aspect with Chiron in Aries, allowing Sagittarians to express their ideas and beliefs with compassion and wisdom. This alignment supports meaningful conversations and offers opportunities for personal growth and healing through communication.

Furthermore, the trine aspect between Venus in Capricorn and Uranus in Taurus on December 2 brings unexpected and exciting developments in the realm of love and relationships. Sagittarians may experience a spark of passion or meet someone who challenges their perspectives and brings refreshing change into their lives.

Love

In matters of the heart, Sagittarius individuals can expect a month of growth, intensity, and surprises. The opposition between Mercury in Sagittarius and Jupiter in Gemini on December 4 creates a magnetic energy, drawing Sagittarians towards intellectual and stimulating connections. They may find themselves attracted to individuals who expand their worldview and ignite their curiosity.

The conjunction between the Sun and Mercury in Sagittarius on December 5 amplifies Sagittarians' communication skills and charm, making them irresistible in love. It's an opportune time for heartfelt conversations, expressing their feelings, and deepening emotional connections with their partners.

The Venus-Uranus trine on December 2 fuels a sense of adventure and excitement in Sagittarius relationships. It encourages them to embrace spontaneity and explore new experiences together. Single Sagittarians may encounter unexpected romantic opportunities or meet someone who challenges their usual preferences, leading to a thrilling and transformative connection.

Career

December presents Sagittarius individuals with opportunities for career advancement and self-discovery. The square aspect between the Sun in Sagittarius and Saturn in Pisces on December 4 brings a sense of discipline and structure to their professional endeavors. Sagittarians are encouraged to embrace responsibility, set realistic goals, and showcase their reliability and dedication.

The sextile between Venus in Capricorn and Neptune in Pisces on December 4 enhances Sagittarians' creative and intuitive abilities. This planetary alignment supports imaginative problem-solving and encourages them to trust their instincts in their career decisions.

Additionally, the Jupiter-Saturn square on December 24 presents Sagittarius individuals with challenges and opportunities for growth. They may encounter obstacles or face changes in their professional path, but by adapting and remaining resilient, they can lay the foundation for future success and advancement.

Finance

Sagittarius individuals are advised to approach their finances with caution and practicality in December. The semi-square aspect between Venus in Aquarius and Saturn in Pisces on December 19 reminds them to make informed decisions and resist impulsive spending. Creating a budget and sticking to it will help maintain financial stability.

The square aspect between Venus in Aquarius and Uranus in Taurus on December 28 brings a need for financial flexibility. Sagittarians should be prepared for unexpected expenses and practice adaptability in managing their resources. Seeking professional advice and maintaining a conservative approach to investments is recommended during this period.

Health

In terms of health and well-being, Sagittarius individuals are encouraged to find balance and prioritize self-care in December. The semi-square aspect between the Sun in Sagittarius and Mars in Leo on December 12 may heighten energy levels and lead to restlessness or impatience. Regular exercise, mindfulness practices, and engaging in activities that promote relaxation will help channel their energy in a positive direction.

The opposition between Venus in Aquarius and Mars in Leo on December 12 may create moments of tension and heightened emotions. It's important for Sagittarians to find healthy outlets for any frustrations or conflicts that arise, whether through open communication or seeking support from loved ones.

Travel

December offers exciting travel prospects for Sagittarius individuals. The biquintile aspect between the Sun and Mars on December 20 ignites a sense of adventure and spontaneity. Sagittarians may find themselves drawn to new destinations or impromptu trips that provide opportunities for personal growth and cultural exploration.

The biquintile aspect between the Sun and Uranus on December 21 further enhances Sagittarians' travel experiences. They may encounter unexpected encounters or detours that add a touch of excitement and novelty to their journeys. Embracing flexibility and being open to new experiences will make their travels memorable and enriching.

Insight from the stars

Embracing change while maintaining a sense of stability is key to navigating the transformative energies of the month. Sagittarians should trust their intuition, communicate their desires openly, and approach their finances with caution.

Best days of the month: December 2nd, 4th, 10th, 19th, 20th, 21st and 31st.